I0017541

Artificial Intelligence for Secondary Schools

A Beginner's Guide

Don Mark Okonkwo

Copyright Notice

All rights reserved. No part of this publication may be reproduced, stored in a retrieval system, or be transmitted, in any form, or by any means, mechanical, electronic, photocopying or otherwise without the prior written consent of the publisher. It is protected under the copyright laws. We prohibit reproduction in whole or part without any written permission.

Copyright © 2025, Don Mark Okonkwo

Artificial Intelligence for Secondary Schools: A Beginner's Guide

ISBN: ISBN: 9798313314204

Cover Design: **Elegantflix**

Published by: Elegant Flix Limited

Address: 10 Abule Parapo Community Road Awoyaya, Ibeju-Lekki, Lagos

Email: elegantflix3dm@gmail.com

Tel: 08131398793

Preface

If you have been following trends in the technology world, you would agree with me that AI is no longer just science fiction thing – it's shaping how we live, learn, and work today. This why I have written this book as your beginner's guide to understanding AI in a simple and engaging way. You don't need to be a computer scientist to explore this field; all you need is curiosity!

In Chapter 1, you'll learn what AI is, how it evolved, and how you already use it daily — think Siri, Netflix recommendations, and smart assistants in your phones and homes.

Chapter 2 breaks down the types of AI. You'll discover how Narrow AI powers tools like spam filters, why General AI is still a dream, and what Super AI could mean for the future.

Chapter 3 takes you inside AI's engine — data, patterns, algorithms, and neural networks. You'll see how AI processes information to become "smart."

In Chapter 4, we'll explore Machine Learning and Deep Learning, the core of AI's intelligence. From self-driving cars to healthcare breakthroughs, you'll see how AI learns and improves.

Chapter 5 highlights how AI is already transforming everyday life—education, healthcare, transportation, and more. It's not just about technology; it's about improving human lives.

If you're interested in coding, Chapter 6 introduces you to Python, the easiest and most popular AI programming language. You'll even try simple AI coding exercises!

But AI isn't just about technology—it raises ethical questions. Chapter 7 discusses fairness, privacy, and bias in AI, and how we can ensure it's used responsibly.

Thinking about an AI career? Chapter 8 explores job opportunities, from AI engineering to robotics. You'll even hear inspiring stories of young AI innovators.

Then, it's time for action! In Chapter 9, you'll build fun AI projects—games, chatbots, and more—giving you hands-on experience.

In Chapter 10, we'll look into AI's future—smarter cities, medical breakthroughs, space exploration, and beyond. You'll learn how you can contribute to AI's evolution.

There are lots of myths about AI. Chapter 11 busts common misconceptions, like the idea that AI thinks like humans or will take over the world.

Finally, Chapter 12 gives you learning resources to continue your AI journey—books, courses, and coding tools to help you grow.

At the end of this book, you'll understand and be better prepared to see and use AI as a tool to shape the future. And that future starts with you.

Are you ready to stay ahead in this future? Then, let's get started!

Table of Contents

Introduction

"You've just done in two
hours what it takes the three
of us two days to do."

My college roommate was working at a retail electronics store in the early 2000s. Occasionally, the store would receive a spreadsheet of thousands of product prices from its competitor. A team of three employees would print the spreadsheet onto a thick stack of paper and split it among themselves. For each product price, they would look up their store's price and note all the products that their competitors sold for less. It usually took a couple of days.

"You know, I could write a program to do that if you have the original file for the printouts," my roommate told them when he saw them sitting on the floor with papers scattered and stacked around them. After a couple of hours, he had a short program that read a competitor's price from a file, found the product in the store's database, and noted whether the competitor was cheaper. The actual program took only a few seconds to run. Because of the speed and efficiency of this programme, my roommate and his co-workers took an extra-long lunch that day.

This is the power of computer programming. A computer is like a Swiss Army knife that you can configure for countless tasks. Many people spend hours clicking and typing to perform repetitive tasks, unaware that the machine they're using could do their job in seconds if they gave it the right instructions.

Why Should You Learn About AI?

AI isn't just for big companies or computer experts— it's for everyone. It's changing how we live, learn, and even solve big problems.

Here's why it matters to you:

- AI can help you study, learn new skills, and even explain things you didn't understand in class.
- Whether it's recommending your next favorite movie or playing games, AI is behind a lot of the fun.
- From self-driving cars to tools that help farmers grow food, AI is making life easier and better for people everywhere.

The coolest thing? AI is still growing, and it needs fresh ideas. That's where you come in. Learning about AI now means you can be part of its future, creating new things and solving problems in ways we haven't even imagined yet.

What You'll Learn in This Book

AI might sound tricky, but don't worry. We're keeping it simple, clear, and fun. By the end of this book, you'll know:

1. **What AI Is**: No confusing words, just easy explanations about what makes AI different from other technology.

2. **How AI Helps Us**: From games to medicine, we'll look at how AI is already making a difference in our world today.
3. **How AI is Made**: You'll learn the basics of coding and even try out Python, one of the main tools used in AI.
4. **Why AI Needs Rules**: We'll discuss why it is important to use AI fairly and avoid mistakes like bias.
5. **What You Can Do With AI**: Want to build your project or plan a career in AI? We'll show you how to get started.

Why This Book is For You

You don't need any experience or special skills to enjoy this book. All you need is a little curiosity and a willingness to explore. The chapters are short, and we'll take things one step at a time.

By the time you finish, you'll have a solid understanding of AI and how you can use it to do amazing things.

Ready to explore the world of AI?

Let's get started!

## CHAPTER 1

What Is Artificial Intelligence?

Artificial intelligence, or AI, might sound like something out of a science fiction movie, but it's a real and exciting field of technology that is transforming the way we live today. At its core, AI is the ability of a machine or a computer system to mimic human intelligence. This means it can perform tasks that usually require human thinking, like learning, problem-solving, and decision-making.

If we decide to go a little deeper into the definition, then AI refers to the simulation of human intelligence in machines that are programmed to think and learn. Unlike regular software, AI can analyze data, recognize patterns, and even make decisions, sometimes better than humans in specific areas.

A Brief History of AI

The concept of AI has been around for decades, with early ideas dating back to ancient myths of intelligent machines. However, AI as a field of study began in the 1950s, when scientists started developing machines capable of logical reasoning. Over the years, AI has grown from simple programs that could play chess to sophisticated systems like Siri, Google Translate, and self-driving cars.

Everyday Examples of AI in Action

AI is already a part of our daily lives, even if we don't always realize it. Here are some examples you might recognize:

- Virtual assistants like Siri and Google Assistant use AI to understand and respond to your voice.

- AI algorithms decide which posts you see based on your interests and activities.
- When websites recommend products, they use AI to analyze what you've browsed or purchased before.
- AI controls the behavior of non-player characters, making games more challenging and realistic.
- AI helps doctors diagnose diseases more accurately and find the best treatments.

Why is AI important?

AI is revolutionizing almost every industry, from healthcare to transportation, education, and entertainment. It helps us solve problems faster, make better decisions, and create new possibilities for the future. By understanding AI, you'll gain a glimpse into how the world works and how you can contribute to shaping it.

Revision Exercise

- List five AI-powered tools or apps you use daily and describe how each one helps you.

What's Next?

Now that you know what AI is and why it matters, we'll go deeper into how it works in the next chapter. You'll learn about the different types of AI and how they're designed to tackle various challenges. This foundational knowledge will set the stage for exploring the building blocks of AI in later chapters.

## CHAPTER 2

Types of AI

Now that you have an idea of what artificial intelligence is, let's break it down a little further. AI isn't just one thing—it comes in different types based on how advanced it is and what it can do. Imagine AI as a ladder, with each type representing a step towards more intelligence.

Let's climb this ladder and get a good grasp of the different steps in it together!

1. Narrow AI: The Everyday Helper

Narrow AI, also known as "weak AI," is the most common type of artificial intelligence we interact with daily. Don't let the term "weak" fool you, though—this type of AI is incredibly powerful at what it does! Narrow AI is designed to perform *one specific task* really well, but that's where its abilities stop. It can't think or act beyond its programmed purpose.

Examples of Narrow AI in Action:

- **Voice Assistants:** Virtual helpers like Siri and Alexa can answer your questions, set reminders, and even tell jokes. But if you ask them to bake a cake, they wouldn't know where to start!
- **Language Translation:** Apps like Google Translate can convert text from one language to another almost instantly. However, they can't jump into a video game and start playing alongside you.
- **Streaming Recommendations:** Platforms like Netflix use AI to analyze your viewing history and suggest movies or shows you might like.

Yet, they can't step in and create a movie for you to watch.

- **Spam Filters:** Email services rely on narrow AI to identify and filter out unwanted spam emails, keeping your inbox clean and organized.
- **Smartphone Cameras:** Many smartphones use AI to enhance photos, automatically adjust lighting, or even suggest the best composition for a shot.

Why is it called 'Narrow AI'?

The term "narrow" is used because this type of AI can only focus on one area. Unlike humans, it doesn't think, learn, or act independently beyond its programming. For example, the AI in a chess game might be unbeatable at chess, but it wouldn't know how to play checkers. This makes it extremely specialized but also limited.

Where Do We See Narrow AI?

Narrow AI is everywhere! It powers the algorithms that recommend your favorite songs on Spotify, predict the weather, and even help doctors identify diseases in medical images. Despite its limited scope, narrow AI plays a huge role in making our lives easier, faster, and more efficient.

2. General AI: The All-Rounder (Not Here Yet)

General AI, also known as "strong AI," is a type of artificial intelligence that scientists and researchers dream of creating. It represents a massive leap forward from the AI we have today. Imagine a robot or computer system that can think, learn, and perform any task a human can do—this is what general AI aims to be. Unlike narrow AI, which excels at one specific task, general AI would be an *all-rounder*, capable of adapting to any situation and solving a wide range of problems.

What Makes General AI Unique?

General AI would not need to be programmed for every specific task. Instead, it would have the ability to learn, reason, and make decisions independently, much like humans do. For example:

- It could solve a complex math problem and then immediately switch to playing football.
- It might write a beautiful poem one moment and then help a doctor diagnose a rare disease the next.

- It could understand emotions and respond with empathy, making it a true conversational partner.

This flexibility is what makes general AI so fascinating—and so challenging to create.

Why Don't We Have General AI Yet?

Creating general AI is incredibly difficult because it requires replicating human-like thinking, learning, and reasoning. Here are some of the main challenges scientists face:

1. **Understanding Intelligence:** We don't fully understand how human intelligence works. How do we learn new things? How do we reason or make decisions in unfamiliar situations? Without answers to these questions, building a machine with the same abilities is tough.

2. **Learning and Adaptability:** Unlike narrow AI, which learns within a limited scope, general AI would need to learn *anything* and adapt to *everything*. This requires creating

machines with a level of flexibility and creativity that we haven't achieved yet.

3. **Ethics and Safety:** A system that can think and act like a human could be very powerful—but also potentially dangerous if it isn't carefully controlled. Scientists need to ensure that general AI will use its abilities responsibly.

What Would General AI Be Capable of Doing?

If we ever succeed in creating general AI, it would completely change the world. Here are some examples of what it might be able to do:

- **Creative Problem Solving:** It could think of solutions to problems humans haven't figured out yet, like curing diseases or solving climate change.
- **Adaptable Work:** A general AI could work in any field—teaching, construction, healthcare, you name it.
- **Human-like Interaction:** It could communicate naturally, understand emotions, and even form relationships with people.

How Is General AI Different From Narrow AI?

To understand how general AI would be different, let's compare it to the narrow AI we use today:

- **Scope:** Narrow AI focuses on one task, like recommending songs or translating languages. General AI would handle any task, just like a human can.
- **Learning:** Narrow AI learns only from specific data. General AI would learn from experience, adapting to new challenges on its own.
- **Reasoning:** Narrow AI follows pre-programmed rules. General AI would think critically and make decisions based on reasoning and creativity.

Where Are We Now?

Currently, general AI is more of a dream than a reality. While scientists and engineers are making progress, we're still in the early stages of understanding what it would take to create such an advanced system. Most of the AI you see today—like Siri, Alexa, or even self-driving cars—falls into the category of narrow AI.

Why Is General AI Important?

The idea of general AI is exciting because it could revolutionize the world. Imagine a future where

- Every problem, no matter how complex, has a solution.
- Machines collaborate with humans to make life better for everyone.
- Work becomes easier, faster, and more efficient across every industry.

At the same time, the journey to creating general AI is also a reminder of how incredible human intelligence really is. It's a frontier that challenges us to think deeply about what it means to be intelligent.

3. Super AI: The Future Vision

Now, let's dream big. Super AI would be an intelligence far beyond what humans can even imagine. Think of it as an AI that's smarter than the smartest person in the world! It could solve problems we don't even know exist yet, like curing all diseases or figuring out how to travel to distant galaxies.

This level of AI is purely science fiction for now, and some experts wonder if it's even possible—or safe. Could we control something so powerful? These are the kinds of questions that make AI both fascinating and a little mysterious.

How AI Gets Smarter

You might be wondering, "How does AI move from one step to another?" The answer lies in data and learning.

- **Narrow AI** learns from specific datasets, like tons of pictures or language patterns.
- For **general AI**, we'd need to teach machines to learn anything, just like a child does.
- **Super AI**? Well, that's something we'll need to figure out along the way!

Why This Matters to You

Understanding the types of AI helps us see how far technology has come and where it's headed. It also helps us think about how to use AI responsibly. For example, if you're designing a new app or project, knowing the difference between narrow and general

AI can guide you in building something practical.

Revision Exercise

- Write a paragraph comparing Narrow AI and General AI. Give one example of each.

What's Next?

In the next chapter, we'll look at how AI works behind the scenes. You'll learn about the magic ingredients—data, algorithms, and patterns—that make AI so smart. By the time we're done, you'll be ready to take on AI concepts like a pro!

## CHAPTER 3

How AI works

Now that you know the types of AI, let's take a closer look at how it all works. You might think AI is magical, but behind the scenes, it's all about data, patterns, and smart programming. In this chapter, we'll break it down step by step so you can understand the building blocks of AI.

1. It All Starts with Data

Imagine you're learning to play a new game, like chess. How do you get better? You practice, pay attention to what works, and avoid making the same mistakes twice. AI learns similarly, but instead of playing games, it works with *data*. Data is the foundation of everything AI does—it's the raw material AI uses to learn and make decisions.

What Is Data?

Data is simply information. It can take many forms, such as:

- **Images:** Photos, like pictures of cats, dogs, or everyday objects.
- **Text:** Written content, such as books, social media posts, or news articles.
- **Numbers:** Statistics, measurements, or financial data, like stock prices.
- **Audio:** Sounds or speech, like recordings of conversations or music.
- **Video:** Moving pictures, like clips showing people walking or animals playing.

Suppose you're training AI to recognize animals. To do this, you need to show thousands of labeled images:

- Pictures of cats labeled as "cat"

- Pictures of dogs labeled as "dog"
  This allows the AI to study what makes a cat different from a dog. The more examples it sees, the better it gets at identifying the patterns that separate one from the other.

Why Is Data So Important?

1. **Learning Patterns:** Data helps AI figure out what's common across many examples. For instance, cats have pointy ears, while dogs might have floppy ears.
2. **Improving Accuracy:** The more data AI processes, the more reliable its decisions become. Imagine learning math with only five problems—you'd struggle! AI, like humans, learns better with more examples.
3. **Handling Variety:** By using diverse data, AI learns to handle different situations. For example, a cat in the dark is still a cat, even if it looks different than one in sunlight.

2. Finding Patterns

Once AI has enough data, it begins to look for *patterns*. Patterns are the key features or traits that help AI make sense of the data.

How Does AI Find Patterns?

AI breaks the data into smaller pieces and examines it for similarities and differences. For example, if you're training AI to recognize cats, it might find patterns like:

- Cats often have triangular, pointy ears.
- Cats have whiskers that stick out from their faces.
- Cats make unique sounds, like meows, and they don't bark like dogs.

By noticing these consistent features, AI learns to associate certain patterns with "cats."

Generalization

One of AI's biggest strengths is its ability to *generalize*. This means that after studying lots of pictures, AI can recognize a cat it has never seen before—even if it's a different color, breed, or in an unusual position. It doesn't memorize specific images; instead, it understands the common traits that define a cat.

3. Algorithms: The Recipe for Learning

At the heart of AI are **algorithms**. An algorithm is like a recipe—a set of instructions that tells the AI how to learn from data and make decisions.

Different Algorithms for Different Tasks

AI uses specific algorithms depending on what it's trying to do. For example:

- **Classification Algorithms:** Sort data into categories. For example, separating emails into "Inbox" or "Spam."
- **Recommendation Algorithms:** Suggest what you might like next, like Netflix recommending shows or YouTube suggesting videos.
- **Natural Language Processing (NLP) Algorithms:** Help AI understand and respond to human language, like when Siri understands your voice commands.

Why are algorithms important?

Algorithms act as the "brains" of AI. They process data, find patterns, and decide what to do next.

Without them, AI wouldn't know how to learn or improve.

4. Neural Networks: Mimicking the Human Brain

One of the coolest things about AI is how it's inspired by the human brain. AI uses something called **neural networks**, which work similarly to how neurons in our brain process information.

How Neural Networks Work

- **Step 1: Breaking Down Information:** Neural networks divide data into tiny pieces. For example, if analyzing an image, they might focus on its edges, colors, or shapes.
- **Step 2: Processing Layers:** The data is passed through several layers, each analyzing it more deeply. Early layers look for basic features, like lines and curves. Later layers combine these features to recognize more complex patterns, like a cat's face.
- **Step 3: Making a Decision:** The network combines everything it learned to make a final prediction or decision, like identifying whether an image shows a cat or a dog.

Let's say the AI analyzes a picture of an animal:

1. The first layer detects basic features like edges and colors.
2. The next layer identifies pointy ears and whiskers.
3. The final layer combines this information and concludes, "This is a cat!"

Why Are Neural Networks So Powerful?

Neural networks are great at handling complex tasks, such as:

- Recognizing faces in photos.
- Translating languages instantly.
- Playing games like chess or Go at a superhuman level.

5. The Role of Machine Learning

You've probably heard the term "machine learning" thrown around a lot. It's one of the key ways that AI learns and improves. Think of machine learning as the process that allows AI to teach itself new things over time instead of just following a fixed set of instructions. It's what makes AI adaptable and capable of handling complex tasks.

How Machine Learning Works

Machine learning is like giving AI a toolkit to figure things out. Instead of telling it every single step to take, you give it the tools and let it learn from experience. This process happens in three main ways:

1. **Supervised Learning:**
   - The AI learns by example.
   - It's like when a teacher shows you how to solve a math problem and gives you the correct answers to practice with.
   - For instance, if you're training AI to recognize apples, you'd show it lots of images labeled "apple" or "not apple." The AI uses these examples to learn what makes an apple an apple.
2. **Unsupervised Learning:**
   - Here, the AI has no labels or answers to start with—it's on its own.
   - It looks at the data and tries to find patterns by itself, like grouping similar things together.
   - For example, an AI looking at a pile of fruit pictures might sort them into groups—

apples, bananas, and oranges—without being told what each fruit is called.

3. **Reinforcement Learning:**
   - The AI learns through trial and error. It tries different things, sees what works, and improves over time.
   - Imagine playing a video game for the first time. You don't know the best moves at the start, but after a few rounds, you figure out strategies that lead to higher scores.
   - For example, an AI controlling a robot might learn how to walk by trying, falling, and gradually getting better with each attempt.

Why Is Machine Learning Important?

- **Continuous Improvement:** Unlike traditional programs, machine learning systems get better with experience. The more data they process, the smarter and more accurate they become.
- **Handling Complexity:** Some tasks—like recognizing faces or translating languages—are too complex to program manually.

Machine learning enables AI to figure these out on its own.

- **Flexibility:** Machine learning allows AI to adapt to new situations. For example, a recommendation system can learn your preferences and suggest better movies or songs over time.

Why It Matters

Machine learning is a game-changer because it allows AI to learn, grow, and adapt. However, it's not perfect. If the data the AI learns from is incomplete, biased, or incorrect, the AI's decisions may also be flawed. This is why understanding how machine learning works is crucial—it helps you see its strengths and limitations.

In the next module, we'll explore machine learning in more detail, explore its types, and examine some real-world examples!

Revision Exercise

- Create a table showing how AI might organize data for a task like recommending movies. Include categories and examples.
- Draw a flow chart showing how an AI system might process data to identify an object in an image.

What's Next?

Now that you know how AI processes data and makes decisions, we'll dive into two special parts of AI: machine learning and deep learning. These are the tools that make AI truly smart. Get ready to explore the cutting-edge techniques that power everything from self-driving cars to language translation apps!

## CHAPTER 4

Machine Learning and Deep Learning

Welcome to one of the most exciting parts of artificial intelligence: *machine learning* and *deep learning*. These two concepts are like the engines that make AI so powerful. But don't worry; you don't need to be a computer scientist to understand them! We'll break everything down in a simple and fun way.

What is Machine Learning?

Imagine you're playing basketball for the first time. At first, your shots might miss the hoop, but as you keep practicing, you notice what works—how to aim, how much force to use, and where to stand. With every attempt, you get better. This is similar to how machine learning works, but instead of a person practicing, it's a computer learning from experience.

Machine learning (ML) teaches computers to improve their performance over time by learning from data. Unlike traditional programming, where we tell a computer exactly what to do, ML allows computers to figure things out on their own.

How It Works:

1. **Data:** The computer is given lots of examples to practice with.
   - For example, pictures of cats and dogs are labeled with their names.
2. **Learning:** The computer finds patterns in the data.
   - It is noticed that cats often have pointy ears and whiskers, while dogs usually don't.
3. **Improvement:** With practice, it gets better at identifying whether a new image shows a cat or a dog.

Everyday Examples:

- **Netflix Recommendations:** ML analyzes the shows you've watched and suggests others you might like.
- **Spam Filters:** Email systems learn to recognize and block unwanted messages.
- **Google Translate:** ML helps translate languages by learning from millions of sentences in different languages.

Types of Machine Learning

Just as there are different ways humans can learn, ML also has different learning methods. Let's dive deeper into the algorithms, explaining how they work and connecting them to real-life examples. We'll also include math to make it clear but simple for secondary school students.

1. Supervised Learning Algorithms

a) Linear Regression

Linear regression is used to predict continuous values, like the price of a house based on its size.

How It Works:

Imagine plotting house sizes on the x-axis and prices on the y-axis. The algorithm draws a straight line that best fits all the points. This line is called the *regression line*, and its equation is:

$$y = mx + c$$

Where:

- y, The predicted value (house price).
- x, The input (house size).
- M, The slope of the line (how much price changes with size).
- c, The y-intercept (the base price when size is 0).

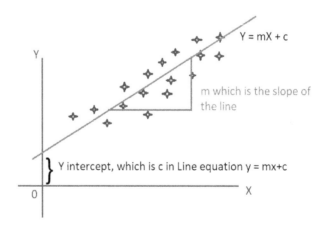

The graph illustrates the equation of a straight line.

Example:

If m=2000 and c=50,000, the price of a 1000 sq. ft. house is:

y=2000(1000)+50,000=2,050,000

The AI adjusts m and c during training to make the line fit the data better.

b) Decision Trees

Decision trees are like a flowchart of questions that lead to a decision.

How It Works:

- Start with all the data.
- Ask a question that splits the data into two or more groups (e.g., "Is the house size > 1000 sq. ft.?").
- Repeat the process for each group until a final decision is reached.

Example:

If you want to decide whether an email is spam or not:

1. Is the email from an unknown sender?
- Yes → Probably spam.
- No → Go to the next question.
2. Does the subject contain "Buy Now"?
- Yes → Spam.
- No → Not spam.

This process creates a tree structure with nodes and branches.

Math Behind Decision Trees:

The algorithm uses **information gain** to choose the best question at each step. Information gain is calculated using **entropy,** which measures uncertainty in the data.

$$\text{Entropy} = -\sum p(x) \log_2 p(x)$$

Where p(x) is the proportion of data in each category. The goal is to reduce entropy at each step.

c) Support Vector Machines (SVM)

SVM is used for classification tasks like identifying cats and dogs.

How It Works:

- The algorithm plots all the data points in a graph.
- It finds a line (or plane in higher dimensions) that separates the categories with the widest possible margin.
- This line is called the **hyperplane.**

Math Behind SVM:

The goal is to maximize the margin between the hyperplane and the nearest data points (support vectors). Mathematically, this is done by minimizing:

$$\text{Minimize } \frac{1}{2}||w||^2$$

Where:

- w: The weights (coefficients of the hyperplane).

- The constraints ensure data points are classified correctly.

2. Unsupervised Learning Algorithms

a) K-Means Clustering

K-Means groups similar data points into clusters.

How It Works:

1. Choose k (the number of clusters).
2. Randomly place k cluster centers (called centroids).
3. Assign each data point to the nearest centroid.
4. Move the centroids to the average position of their assigned points.
5. Repeat steps 3 and 4 until the centroids stop moving.

Example:

Suppose you have data on students' grades in math and science. K-Means might group them into clusters of:

- High math, high science.
- High math, low science.
- Low math, low science.

Math Behind K-Means:

The algorithm minimizes the total distance between points and their cluster center:

$$\text{Minimize} \sum_{i=1}^{n} \sum_{j=1}^{k} ||x_i - c_j||^2$$

Where:

- xi: Data points.
- CJ: Cluster centers.

b) Principal Component Analysis (PCA)

PCA reduces the number of features in data while preserving as much information as possible.

How It Works:

1. Find the directions (principal components) where the data varies the most.
2. Project the data onto these components to reduce its dimensions.

Example:

If you have 3D data (x, y, z), PCA might reduce it to 2D by finding the plane that captures the most variation.

Math Behind PCA:

PCA uses **eigenvectors** and **eigenvalues** to find principal components. The eigenvector with the largest eigenvalue is the direction of maximum variance.

3. Reinforcement Learning Algorithms

a) Q-Learning

Q-learning is used for decision-making in environments like games.

How It Works:

- The AI learns by trying different actions and getting rewards or penalties.
- It keeps a table of Q(s,a), which is the value of taking action aaa in state sss.
- The AI updates the table using the formula:

$$Q(s,a) = Q(s,a) + \alpha[r + \gamma \max_a Q(s',a') - Q(s,a)]$$

Where:

- α: Learning rate.
- r, Reward for the action.
- γ: Discount factor (how much future rewards matter).

Example:

In a maze, the AI learns the best path to the exit by trying different routes and remembering which ones lead to success.

b) Deep Q-Networks (DQN)

DQN extends Q-Learning using deep learning to handle complex environments.

How It Works:

- Instead of a table, the AI uses a neural network to approximate $Q(s,a)$.
- This allows it to handle environments with many possible states, like video games.

4. How Do Machines Learn from Data?

Let's break down the process of teaching a machine to recognize apples and oranges:

1. **Output Data:** You collect lots of labeled pictures of apples and oranges.
2. **Training:** The AI studies the images to find patterns (e.g., apples are red and smooth, oranges are orange and textured).
3. **Testing:** You show the AI new, unlabeled pictures and check if it can identify them correctly.
4. **Improvement:** If it makes mistakes, you adjust its algorithms or give it more data to learn from.

The more data you give the AI, the better it gets at identifying new apples and oranges accurately.

5. Real-World Applications of Machine Learning and Deep Learning

Here are some amazing ways ML and DL are changing the world:

- **Voice Assistants:** Alexa, Siri, and Google Assistant understand and respond to your voice.
- **Self-Driving Cars:** These vehicles use deep learning to recognize roads, signs, and other vehicles.

- **Healthcare:** AI helps doctors detect diseases like cancer by analyzing medical images.
- **Gaming:** AI game opponents learn to play better by observing player strategies.
- **Finance:** ML detects fraud by spotting unusual patterns in transactions.

6. Challenges and Limitations

While ML and DL are powerful, they're not without challenges.

1. **Data Quantity:** AI needs a lot of data to learn effectively.
2. **Data Quality:** If the data is biased or incorrect, the AI's decisions will also be flawed.
3. **Computing Power:** Training AI models can require significant computational resources.
4. **Interpretability:** Sometimes, it's hard to understand why AI makes certain decisions, especially in deep learning models.

Revision Exercise

- Write down one example each of supervised, unsupervised, and reinforcement learning. Explain how the AI learns in each case.

What's Next?

Now that you understand how machine learning and deep learning work, we'll now go on and study how AI is making an impact in the real world. In the next chapter, we'll examine how AI is transforming industries like education, entertainment, and healthcare.

## CHAPTER 5

AI in Our Lives

Artificial Intelligence (AI) has woven itself into the fabric of our daily lives, often so seamlessly that we hardly notice it. Whether you're learning at school, playing your favorite video game, binge-watching shows, or even tracking your health, AI is working behind the scenes to make life smarter, more convenient, and more exciting.

In this chapter we're going to explore the real-world applications of AI in detail.

AI in Education

AI is revolutionizing the way students learn by adapting to individual needs.

Here's how:

1. Adaptive Learning Platforms

- Platforms like Khan Academy, Duolingo, and Quizlet use AI to assess how well you're doing with a subject.
- **How it works:** If you struggle with algebra, the AI identifies this and slows down, offering simpler explanations or additional exercises. Once you master the basics, it increases the difficulty level.
- **Why it matters:** Every student learns differently. With AI, education becomes tailored to your pace and style, ensuring you don't get left behind.

2. Virtual Assistants

- Tools like Google Assistant, Alexa, and Siri act as digital helpers.

- **Real-life example:** You can ask, "What's the capital of France?" or "Set a reminder for my math homework at 5 PM," and they respond instantly.
- These AI assistants don't just answer questions—they learn from your queries to improve their accuracy over time.

3. AI-Enhanced Teaching

- Teachers benefit too! AI automates grading tasks for quizzes and assignments, freeing up their time to focus on teaching.
- Advanced AI tools also analyze student performance to identify patterns, helping teachers pinpoint areas where students need extra help.

Impact: With AI, classrooms are evolving into dynamic spaces where both teachers and students have access to tools that make learning more efficient and enjoyable.

AI in Entertainment

AI enhances entertainment by making it more engaging, personalized, and creative.

1. Smart Recommendations

- **Netflix and YouTube** use AI to recommend what you should watch next.
- **How it works:** These platforms track what you've already watched, analyze the genres or themes you enjoy, and suggest similar content.
- **Example:** If you just finished watching a superhero movie, Netflix might suggest other action-packed blockbusters.

2. Personalized Music

- **Spotify** uses AI to understand your music taste and create custom playlists like "Discover Weekly."
- **How it works:** It analyzes your listening history, compares it to other users' habits, and introduces songs you're likely to enjoy.

3. Gaming with AI

- In games like Minecraft, Fortnite, or The Sims, AI powers non-playable characters (NPCs) to make them behave intelligently.

- **Example:** In Fortnite, an NPC might dodge your attacks or sneak up on you strategically, making the game more challenging and fun.
- AI even enables players to have more immersive virtual reality (VR) experiences by creating realistic environments and opponents.

Impact: AI makes entertainment not just a one-size-fits-all experience but something uniquely crafted for you, whether it's a playlist, movie recommendation, or gaming challenge.

AI in Healthcare

AI isn't just about fun—it plays a crucial role in improving health and saving lives.

1. Early Diagnosis

- AI systems can analyze medical images (like X-rays or MRIs) to detect diseases, such as cancer, earlier than a doctor might.
- **How it works:** AI algorithms are trained on thousands of images to recognize patterns that signal a problem. For instance, an AI

might detect a tiny shadow on an X-ray that indicates early-stage lung cancer.

2. Personalized Medicine

- AI helps doctors create treatment plans tailored to an individual's specific genetic makeup and medical history.
- **Example:** AI might suggest a different dosage or type of medication for two patients with the same disease based on how their bodies are likely to respond.

3. Health Monitoring

- Devices like smartwatches and fitness trackers (e.g., Fitbit or Apple Watch) use AI to monitor your activity, heart rate, and even sleep patterns.
- **Example:** If your watch notices irregular heartbeats, it might warn you to seek medical advice before a serious condition develops.

Impact: AI in healthcare is not just reactive—it's proactive, helping doctors and individuals prevent issues before they escalate.

AI in Transportation

AI is transforming how we move, making travel faster, safer, and more efficient.

1. Self-Driving Cars

- Companies like Tesla, Waymo, and Cruise are developing vehicles that use AI to drive without human input.
- **How it works:** Cameras, sensors, and AI algorithms allow these cars to "see" the road, recognize pedestrians, and even predict the actions of other drivers.
- **Example:** If a ball rolls into the street, an AI-powered car might anticipate that a child could follow and stop immediately.

2. Navigation Apps

- Apps like Google Maps and Waze use AI to calculate the fastest routes and update them in real time based on traffic conditions.
- **Example:** If there's a traffic jam on your usual route, Google Maps suggests an alternate path.

3. Smarter Public Transport

- AI helps optimize bus and train schedules by analyzing data on passenger numbers, traffic patterns, and delays.

Impact: AI isn't just getting us from A to B; it's doing so more safely and efficiently, reducing accidents and travel times.

AI's Bigger Picture

From helping you with schoolwork to saving lives in hospitals and revolutionizing how we travel, AI is reshaping the world in ways we couldn't have imagined a few decades ago. But with all its benefits, it's important to remember that AI is a tool—its power depends on how we use it.

As we move forward, learning about AI isn't just exciting; it's essential. By understanding how it works, you can use it wisely and even shape its future.

Revision Exercise

- Find an AI-powered learning app, try it out, and write a short review of your experience

- List three ways AI is used in healthcare and describe how it improves patient care.

What's Next?

In the next chapter, we'll pull back the curtain to see how AI is built, from programming languages like Python to the basic steps in coding AI systems. Whether you dream of building your own AI or just want to understand it better, this journey is just beginning. Let's dive in!

## CHAPTER 6

Building Blocks of AI

AI might seem like a futuristic technology, but it's built on tools and concepts that anyone can learn. In this chapter, we'll dive into the programming languages behind AI, get hands-on with Python, and understand the coding concepts that power intelligent systems.

Let's start building!

Programming Languages Used in AI

AI relies on programming languages to "talk" to computers. Here are some popular ones:

- **Python**: Known for its simplicity, flexibility, and rich library ecosystem (like NumPy, TensorFlow, and PyTorch), Python is the top choice for AI beginners and experts alike.
- **Java**: Often used in large-scale systems, such as finance and enterprise applications that integrate AI.
- **R**: Favored by data scientists for analyzing, visualizing, and modeling data.
- **C++**: Used for performance-heavy tasks, like game development and AI in robotics.
- **JavaScript**: Essential for web-based AI applications like chatbots.

Since **Python** is beginner-friendly and powerful for AI, we'll focus on that in this chapter!

Getting Started with Python

Python is like a universal language for AI. Here are some beginner-friendly Python examples to help you understand how AI "thinks."

1. Displaying Information

Use Python to display text or results.

Python code

```
print("Hello, AI World!")
```

- **What it does:** Displays the message "Hello, AI World!".
- **Why it matters:** Printing is essential for seeing results and debugging your code.

2. Simple Math

AI often uses math to analyze data or make decisions.

Python code

```
x = 5

y = 3

result = x + y

print("The sum is:", result)
```

- **What it does:** Adds 5 and 3, stores the result in the result variable, and displays: The sum is: 8.
- **Why it matters:** AI systems use similar calculations to process and analyze data.

3. Making Decisions

AI often makes decisions based on conditions.

Python code

```python
score = 85

if score > 50:

    print("You passed!")

else:

    print("You failed.")
```

What it does: It checks if the score is greater than 50. If true, it prints, You passed!. Otherwise, it prints, 'You failed'.

- **Why it matters:** AI uses conditionals to make decisions, such as recommending movies or detecting spam emails.

Learning Python with AI-Related Examples
---

4. Loops: Repeating Actions

AI often processes large amounts of data by repeating tasks.

Python code

```
for i in range(5):

    print("Training AI... Step", i + 1)
```

- **What it does:** Prints the phrase "Training AI... Step X" five times, where X is the step number.
- **Why it matters:** Loops are used in AI to train models by repeating tasks thousands or millions of times.

5. Functions: Reusable Code

AI uses functions to break down tasks into smaller, reusable steps.

Python code

```
def greet(name):

    return f"Hello, {name}!"

print(greet("Student"))
```

- **What it does:** Defines a function greet that takes a name and returns a greeting message.
- **Why it matters:** Functions allow AI systems to handle repetitive tasks more efficiently.

6. Analyzing Data (Lists and Loops)

AI often works with lists of data.

Python code

```
temperatures = [22, 25, 20, 19, 23]

average_temp = sum(temperatures) / len(temperatures)

for temp in temperatures:

    print(f"Temperature: {temp}°C")

print(f"Average Temperature: {average_temp}°C")
```

- **What it does:**
    ⇒ Stores daily temperatures in a list.
    ⇒ Calculates the average temperature.
    ⇒ Loops through the list to print each temperature.
- **Why it matters:** AI analyzes large datasets (like weather patterns or user preferences) using lists and loops.

7. Predicting Outcomes (Simple If-Else Example)

AI predicts outcomes based on rules or data patterns.

Python code

```python
weather = "sunny"

if weather == "sunny":

    print("Wear sunglasses!")

elif weather == "rainy":

    print("Take an umbrella.")

else:

    print("Stay prepared for any weather.")
```

- **What it does:**
  - ⇒ Checks the value of the weather and prints a message based on its condition.
- **Why it matters:** AI systems use similar logic to provide recommendations (e.g., suggesting clothes based on the weather forecast).

Building Simple AI Features

8. Making Predictions (Simulating AI Behavior)

Let's simulate how AI predicts outcomes based on a dataset.

Python code

```
data = [60, 65, 70, 75, 80]  # Student scores

threshold = 70

for score in data:

    if score >= threshold:

        print(f"Score {score}: Pass")
```

```
else:

    print(f"Score {score}: Fail")
```

- **What it does:**
  - ⇒ Checks each score in the list.
  - ⇒ If the score is above or equal to 70, it prints "Pass"; otherwise, it prints "Fail."
- **Why it matters:** AI uses thresholds and conditions to classify data, like determining if an email is spam.

9. Training and Testing (Simulating AI Learning)

Python code

```
training_data = ["cat", "dog", "cat", "cat", "dog"]

new_data = ["cat", "dog", "bird"]

for item in new_data:

  if item in training_data:

    print(f"{item}: Recognized!")

  else:

    print(f"{item}: Unknown!")
```

- **What it does:**
  - ⇒ Trains the AI with a dataset of known items.
  - ⇒ Compares new data to the training data and identifies what it recognizes.
- **Why it matters:** AI systems learn from training data and use that knowledge to make predictions on unseen data.

Revision Exercise

- Write a short Python program that asks the user for their name and greets them.

What's Next?

Understanding these coding basics is like opening the door to AI's world. Each concept—variables, loops, conditionals, and functions—forms the foundation of how AI operates. By practicing these ideas in Python, you'll be ready to create more complex AI projects.

In the next chapter, we'll explore an important topic: **ethics in AI**. Why are fairness, privacy, and responsibility critical when creating AI systems? Let's go deeper!

## CHAPTER 7

Ethics in AI

AI holds incredible potential to transform the world, but with this power comes the responsibility to use it wisely. In this chapter into the ethical challenges of AI and why they matter to everyone, especially young innovators like you.

An understanding of these issues is critical, because it will help us build smarter systems that respect fairness, privacy, and safety.

Why Ethics is Important in AI

Ethics in AI ensures that we create systems that are trustworthy, responsible, and beneficial to society. Imagine a self-driving car faced with a moral dilemma:

- Should it swerve to avoid a pedestrian, risking the safety of the passengers?
- Or should it prioritize the passengers and potentially harm others?

Such decisions highlight the need for ethical guidelines in AI.

The Role of Ethics

Ethics in AI helps us:

1. **Build Trust**: People need to feel confident that AI systems will work fairly and reliably. Without trust, innovations like autonomous cars or AI-driven healthcare won't gain acceptance.
2. **Protect Privacy:** AI often works with sensitive personal information. It's crucial to ensure that this data is collected, stored, and used responsibly.

3. **Ensure Fairness:** AI must treat everyone equally, without bias or discrimination, to avoid reinforcing inequalities in society.

When we include these ethical considerations into AI development, we can ensure that technology serves everyone, not just a select few.

Key Ethical Challenges in AI

1. Bias in AI

AI systems learn from data, and if that data is biased, the AI can replicate and amplify these biases.

Example:
An AI tool for hiring might favor men over women if it's trained on historical hiring data where men were preferred.

Solution:

- Use diverse, balanced datasets to train AI models.
- Regularly test AI for fairness by checking its decisions against real-world scenarios.

- Encourage inclusive teams of developers to bring different perspectives into the design process.

2. Privacy Concerns

AI systems often collect vast amounts of data to function effectively. But what happens if this data is misused or stolen?

Example:
Social media platforms collect user data to recommend posts or ads. However, this data could be exploited to invade your privacy.

Solution:

- Create strict rules for how companies collect, store, and use data.
- Develop AI that minimizes data collection, only storing what is absolutely necessary.

3. Transparency in AI

AI decisions can feel like they come from a "black box." Users often don't know how or why a decision was made.

Example:

An AI denies a loan application, but the applicant doesn't know why.

Solution:

- Build **explainable AI** (XAI) that makes decisions in a way people can understand
- Use visual tools, like graphs or charts, to show how AI reached its conclusion.

Real-World Examples of Ethical Dilemmas in AI

1. Facial Recognition

- **The Issue**: Facial recognition systems are used for security and identification, but they can misidentify people, especially in diverse populations.
- **Ethical Concern**: Misidentifications can lead to wrongful arrests or violations of privacy.
- **Solution**: Developers must rigorously test these systems on diverse datasets and create policies limiting their misuse.

2. Social Media Algorithms

- **The Issue**: AI determines what content you see online.
- **Ethical Concern**: These algorithms can create "echo chambers," where users only see opinions they already agree with, which may deepen divisions in society.
- **Solution**: Platforms should design algorithms to show diverse perspectives and help users make informed choices.

3. AI in Healthcare

- **The Issue**: AI systems help diagnose diseases, but what if they make a mistake?
- **Ethical Concern**: Who is responsible for errors—the AI's developer or the doctor who used it?
- **Solution**: Developers should provide clear guidelines on how to use AI tools, and AI should always be supervised by trained professionals.

Your Role in Shaping Ethical AI

As a future AI innovator, you have the power to make a positive impact. Here's how you can approach ethics in AI:

1. **Think Before You Code**: Always ask, *Who could this AI help, and who could it harm?* Thinking critically helps you spot potential risks.
2. **Learn About Fairness:** Study how to identify and avoid bias in data and algorithms. For example, when training AI, check if your data represents all groups equally.
3. **Be Responsible:** Respect privacy and transparency in every project you work on. Always consider how your AI impacts users.

A Simple Example of Ethical AI Thinking

Imagine creating an AI tool that helps students choose careers:

Questions to Ask:

- Does my AI suggest careers fairly to both boys and girls?
- Does it consider students from different backgrounds?
- Can I explain why the AI made specific recommendations?

By thinking about these questions, you're already taking steps toward ethical AI.

Revision Exercise

- Write arguments for and against using AI for facial recognition in public spaces.

What's Next?

Ethics in AI is not just about solving technical problems—it's about creating a better world for everyone. By focusing on fairness, privacy, and transparency, you can help build AI systems that people trust and value.

In the next chapter, we'll explore the **exciting career opportunities in AI**. From becoming a data scientist to building robots, the possibilities are endless. Get ready to dream big and start planning your future in the world of AI.

CHAPTER 8

Careers in AI

Artificial Intelligence is revolutionizing industries and opening doors to incredible career opportunities. Whether you're fascinated by cutting-edge technology, driven to solve global challenges, or excited about creating smarter apps and robots, AI has a career path for you.

In this chapter, we'll explore some of the most exciting AI roles, how to prepare for them, and hear inspiring stories of young people already making an impact.

Exciting AI-Related Careers

AI touches nearly every field, from healthcare and transportation to entertainment and education. Let's dive into the most in-demand careers in AI and what makes them so exciting.

1. Data Scientist

What They Do: Data scientists analyze and interpret massive amounts of data, uncovering patterns that help companies make better decisions. They combine statistics, programming, and AI tools to find meaningful insights.

Example: A data scientist at an online retailer might use AI to predict which products will be trending next season, helping the company stock up before demand peaks.

Why It's Cool:

- You turn raw data into actionable insights.
- Every project directly impacts the real world, from saving costs to launching new products.

2. AI Engineer

What They Do: AI engineers design and build AI systems, from virtual assistants like Alexa to self-driving cars. They write the code that powers intelligent machines and ensure these systems work efficiently.

Example: An AI engineer might create an algorithm that helps a self-driving car recognize traffic signals, pedestrians, and other vehicles on the road.

Why It's Cool:

- You work on futuristic technologies that were once only in sci-fi movies.
- Your innovations can transform industries, making life easier and safer.

3. Machine Learning Researcher

What They Do: Machine learning researchers push the boundaries of AI by developing new algorithms and improving how machines learn from data. They are the scientists behind breakthroughs like ChatGPT and AI-powered medical diagnoses.

Example: A machine learning researcher might design an AI system that can outperform humans in complex strategy games like chess or Go, paving the way for more advanced problem-solving applications.

Why It's Cool:

- You get to experiment and innovate at the cutting edge of AI.
- Your work lays the foundation for technologies of the future.

4. AI Ethicist

What They Do: AI ethicists ensure that AI systems are fair, safe, and aligned with human values. They address issues like bias, transparency, and the responsible use of AI.

Example: An AI ethicist might review a hiring algorithm to ensure it doesn't favor certain candidates based on gender or race.

Why It's Cool:

- You get to shape how AI impacts society.
- Your work ensures that AI benefits everyone, not just a select few.

5. Robotics Engineer

What They Do: Robotics engineers combine AI with mechanical engineering to create robots that can think, learn, and interact with their environment.

Example: A robotics engineer might design a drone that uses AI to deliver packages autonomously, navigating through crowded cities without human help.

Why It's Cool:

- You bring machines to life, creating technology that moves and acts in the real world.
- Your creations can perform tasks humans find too dangerous, difficult, or time-consuming.

How Students Can Prepare for a Career in AI

No matter where you're starting, there are practical steps you can take to build a strong foundation in AI.

1. Learn the Basics of Coding

Coding is the language of AI. Start with beginner-friendly programming languages like Python.

Tips to Get Started:

- Write simple programs, like a calculator or a chatbot.
- Try free online tutorials on websites like Codecademy or Khan Academy.

2. Master Math and Science

AI relies heavily on math and science, so focus on subjects like:

- **Algebra**: For understanding algorithms.
- **Statistics**: To analyze and interpret data.
- **Physics**: For robotics and simulations.

3. Experiment with AI Tools

There are plenty of tools designed to help beginners explore AI concepts:

- **Scratch**: Perfect for younger students learning coding basics.
- **Teachable Machine by Google**: A fun, interactive way to train your own AI models.

4. Participate in Competitions

Competitions like coding hackathons or robotics challenges are great for building skills and meeting like-minded peers.

- Examples: **FIRST Robotics**, **Codeforces**, or **AI4ALL programs**.

5. Stay Curious and Keep Learning

AI is constantly evolving, so keep exploring!

- Watch videos, read books, or take online courses on platforms like Coursera or Udemy.
- Follow AI news to stay updated on the latest breakthroughs.

Inspiring Stories of Young AI Innovators

Emma Yang

- **Achievement**: Emma created an app called *Timeless* to help Alzheimer's patients recognize their loved ones using AI-powered facial recognition.
- **Her Journey**: She started coding at age 8 and combined her passion for technology with her desire to help others.

Tanmay Bakshi

- **Achievement**: Tanmay became a coding prodigy by age 5 and now works on AI projects to improve healthcare systems.
- **His Advice**: *"Learn by doing—start small and dream big."*

Every great AI innovator starts somewhere. Your journey could lead you to build life-changing technologies, solve global problems, or create the next big AI breakthrough.

Your AI Career Path Awaits

AI is shaping the future, and you have the potential to play a key role. Whether your passion lies in building intelligent systems, designing robots, or ensuring AI is ethical, there's a career path for you. With curiosity, dedication, and the right skills, you can turn your dreams into reality.

Revision Exercise

- Choose one AI-related career and write a short description of what someone in that role does.

- Make a list of skills (e.g., coding, problem-solving) that are important for AI jobs. Highlight the ones you already have.

What's Next?

Now that you've explored careers in AI, it's time to get hands-on! In the next chapter, we'll guide you through fun, beginner-friendly AI projects where you can unleash your creativity and build something amazing. Let's get started!

## CHAPTER 9

Fun AI Projects for Beginners

AI is fascinating and fun, and you don't need advanced skills to dive in. In this chapter, we'll explore beginner-friendly AI projects that combine creativity with learning. These projects range from games to practical tools and even encourage you to think about how AI can solve real-world problems.

AI-Powered Games and Simple Tools

Here are a few exciting projects you can try. Each idea is simple to understand and implement but offers endless possibilities for customization and improvement

1. Rock-Paper-Scissors Game with AI

In this project, you'll create an AI that learns to play *rock-paper-scissors*. It will try to predict your next move based on patterns in your previous choices.

How It Works:

- The player chooses rock, paper, or scissors.
- The AI "learns" from the player's past moves and predicts their next choice.

Python Code Example:

Python code

```python
import random

# List of possible moves

moves = ["rock", "paper", "scissors"]

# History to store player's choices

player_moves = []

def ai_predict():
```

```python
    if not player_moves:
        # Random choice if no history is available
        return random.choice(moves)
    # Predict based on player's last move
    return random.choice([move for move in moves if
move != player_moves[-1]])

def get_winner(player, ai):
    if player == ai:
        return "It's a tie!"
    elif (player == "rock" and ai == "scissors") or

(player == "paper" and ai == "rock") or

        (player == "scissors" and ai == "paper"):
        return "You win!"
    else:
        return "AI wins!"

# Game loop
```

```python
while True:

    player = input("Enter rock, paper, or scissors (or
'quit' to stop): ").lower()

    if player == "quit":

        print("Thanks for playing!")

        break

    elif player not in moves:

        print("Invalid input. Try again.")

        continue

    ai = ai_predict()

    print(f"AI chose: {ai}")

    result = get_winner(player, ai)

    print(result)

    # Update history

    player_moves.append(player)
```

What You'll Learn:

⇒ How AI can use history to make predictions.

⇒ Basic game mechanics and player interaction.

2. Mood Detector

In this project, you'll build an AI tool that guesses someone's mood based on text they enter. It uses sentiment analysis, a popular natural language processing (NLP) technique.

How It Works:

⇒ The user types a message.

⇒ The AI analyzes the sentiment (positive, neutral, or negative) and guesses the mood.

Python Code Example (Using TextBlob):

Python code

```python
from textblob import TextBlob

def detect_mood(text):

    analysis = TextBlob(text)

# Polarity: Negative (<0), Neutral (0), Positive (>0)

    if analysis.sentiment.polarity > 0:
```

```python
        return "You seem happy! ☺"

    elif analysis.sentiment.polarity < 0:

        return "You seem upset. ☹"

    else:

        return "You seem neutral. ☺"

# Test the mood detector

while True:

    text = input"How are you feeling today? (Type 'quit' to exit): ")

    if text.lower() == "quit":

        print("Goodbye!")

        break

    mood = detect_mood(text)

    print(mood)
```

What You'll Learn:

⇒ How sentiment analysis works.
⇒ Using external libraries to perform NLP tasks.

3. Chatbot Friend

Create a chatbot that interacts with users. It can answer questions, tell jokes, or suggest study tips.

How It Works:

⇒ The chatbot uses simple keyword matching to understand and respond.

⇒ You can later expand it with AI-powered tools like OpenAI's GPT models.

Python Code Example:

Python code

```python
def chatbot_response(user_input):

    # Simple responses

    responses = {

"hello": "Hi there! How can I help you today?"

"joke": "Why don't scientists trust atoms? Because they make up everything! 😄"

"study tips": "Start with small, focused sessions and take short breaks. You've got this!"
```

```python
    "bye": "Goodbye! Have a great day!"

}

    # Check for a keyword in the user's input

for keyword in responses:

    if keyword in user_input.lower():

        return responses[keyword]

    return "I'm not sure how to respond to that. Can
you try asking something else?"

# Chat loop

print("Chatbot: Hi! I'm your friendly chatbot. Type
'bye' to exit.")

while True:

    user_input = input("You: ")

    if "bye" in user_input.lower():

        print("Chatbot: Bye! Take care.")

        break

    print("Chatbot:", chatbot_response(user_input))
```

What You'll Learn:

⇒ Basic natural language understanding (NLU).

⇒ How chatbots interact with users.

Encouraging Creativity with AI

- **Combine Projects**: Blend the chatbot with the mood detector for a more interactive experience.
- **Solve Problems**: Think of practical uses for your projects, like a chatbot for mental health support or a tool for learning new vocabulary.
- **Personalize**: Add your unique style, like custom messages, themes, or sounds.

Sharing Your Creations

- **With Friends and Family**: Let them test your projects and share their thoughts.
- **Online AI Communities**: Platforms like GitHub or forums like Reddit's r/learnprogramming are great for sharing and improving your work.
- **Local Events**: Join coding hackathons or school tech fairs to showcase your skills.

Revision Exercise

- Design a simple chatbot using pseudocode or a Python script.

What's Next?

Great job experimenting with these AI projects! You've taken your first steps into the exciting world of AI. In the next chapter, we'll explore **The Future of AI** and discuss how this technology will shape the world—and your role in its development. Get ready to dream big!

## CHAPTER 10

The Future of AI

What will the world look like in the next 10, 20, or even 50 years? One thing is certain: artificial intelligence (AI) will play a major role in shaping it. As AI continues to evolve, it promises to revolutionize industries, solve complex problems, and create new opportunities for humanity. But it also raises important questions such as:

⇒ How will AI transform our lives?
⇒ What responsibilities do we have as innovators?

⇒ And how can students prepare for an AI-powered future?

Let's examine how AI is changing the world today, what its future potential looks like, and how you can play an essential role in guiding this transformation.

How AI is Changing the World Today

Artificial intelligence is already making a significant impact in various areas of life, from healthcare to education, transportation to environmental conservation. Let's take a closer look at how AI is shaping the present.

1. Healthcare

AI is revolutionizing healthcare by improving diagnostics, personalizing treatments, and assisting in surgeries.

- **Diagnosing Diseases Faster and More Accurately:** AI algorithms analyze medical data—such as X-rays, MRIs, and genetic profiles—to identify patterns that doctors might miss. This allows for earlier detection of diseases like cancer, diabetes, and Alzheimer's.

Example: AI tools like IBM Watson Health help doctors diagnose conditions and suggest treatment options based on vast amounts of medical literature.

- **Robotic-Assisted Surgeries:** AI-powered robots assist surgeons in performing complex procedures with unmatched precision, reducing the risk of human error and improving patient outcomes.
Example: The da Vinci Surgical System enables minimally invasive surgeries with smaller incisions, less pain, and faster recovery times for patients.

- **Drug Discovery:** AI accelerates the development of new medicines by analyzing millions of chemical compounds to predict which ones might be effective against specific diseases.

2. Education

AI is transforming how we learn by providing personalized experiences, supporting teachers, and making education more accessible.

- **Personalized Learning Experiences:** AI-powered tools adapt lessons to a student's unique needs, identifying their strengths and weaknesses to create a tailored learning plan. **Example.** Platforms like Khan Academy use AI to recommend practice exercises based on a student's progress.
- **Virtual Tutors:** AI tutors provide one-on-one assistance to students, answering questions, explaining concepts, and offering additional resources.
  Example: Apps like Photomath allow students to take a picture of a math problem and receive step-by-step guidance.
- **Bridging Accessibility Gaps:** AI tools translate text, provide subtitles for videos, and convert written content into audio for students with disabilities.

3. Transportation

AI is improving the way we travel by making transportation safer, more efficient, and environmentally friendly.

- **Self-Driving Cars:** Autonomous vehicles use AI to process data from cameras, sensors, and maps, enabling them to navigate roads safely without human intervention. **Example:** Companies like Tesla and Waymo are developing cars that can park themselves, detect obstacles, and drive autonomously.

- **Optimizing Public Transportation:** AI helps cities design better transit systems by predicting traffic patterns, optimizing bus routes, and reducing delays. **Example:** In Singapore, AI-powered systems analyze traffic data to adjust traffic lights in real time, reducing congestion and travel times.

4. Environment

AI is being used to protect the planet and address environmental challenges.

- **Monitoring Deforestation and Wildlife:** AI analyzes satellite imagery and drone footage to detect illegal logging and track endangered species. **Example:** Conservationists use AI-powered tools to monitor animal populations and identify threats like poaching or habitat destruction.

- **Reducing Energy Waste:** Smart systems powered by AI optimize energy use in homes and cities, minimizing waste and lowering carbon emissions. **Example:** AI adjusts lighting, heating, and cooling systems in buildings based on occupancy and weather conditions, saving energy and costs.

Speculations on the Future of AI

The future of AI holds endless possibilities. As technology advances, it will create new opportunities, industries, and ways of living. Here are some exciting predictions for the future of AI:

1. Smarter Cities

AI could transform urban living by making cities more efficient, sustainable, and livable.

- AI systems could manage traffic in real time, reducing congestion and improving air quality.

- Smart waste management systems could sort and recycle trash automatically, minimizing landfill use.
- Sensors and AI algorithms could monitor infrastructure like bridges and roads, predicting maintenance needs before problems occur.

2. Advanced Healthcare

AI will continue to push the boundaries of what's possible in medicine:

- AI systems might predict illnesses before symptoms appear by analyzing trends in health data from wearable devices. **Example:** Smartwatches could alert users to potential heart problems or changes in blood sugar levels, allowing for early intervention.
- Personalized medicine will become a reality, with AI creating treatments tailored to an individual's genetic profile and lifestyle.

3. Space Exploration

AI-powered robots and systems will play a vital role in exploring the universe.

- Robots equipped with AI could navigate hostile environments on distant planets, collecting data and searching for signs of life. **Example:** NASA's Perseverance Rover already uses AI to traverse the Martian landscape, and future missions might include robots capable of building habitats for humans.
- AI could optimize spacecraft routes, reducing travel time and energy use for interstellar missions.

4. New Jobs and Industries

Just as the internet created entirely new professions, AI will open doors to careers and industries we can't yet imagine:

- **AI Ethics Auditors:** Professionals who ensure AI systems are fair, transparent, and responsible.
- **Virtual Reality Architects:** designers who use AI to create immersive digital experiences.
- **AI-Augmented Artists:** Creatives who collaborate with AI to produce music, art, and literature.

The Role Students Can Play in Shaping This Future

As students, you are not just spectators in AI's journey—you are its future creators, leaders, and advocates. Here's how you can play an active role in shaping the future of AI:

1. Be Responsible Innovators

- Think critically about the impact of your AI projects. Ask questions like:
- "Could this AI harm someone unintentionally?"
- "Is my AI system fair and unbiased?"
- "Does this technology respect people's privacy?"
- Ensure that the AI tools you build are ethical, inclusive, and beneficial for society.

2. Stay Curious and Keep Learning

- AI is constantly evolving, and staying updated on the latest advancements is crucial. **How to Stay Informed:**
- Take online courses in AI and machine learning.

- Experiment with tools like Python libraries (e.g., TensorFlow, PyTorch, or Scikit-learn).
- Participate in AI hackathons or competitions to practice your skills.

3. Collaborate and Share Ideas

- Collaboration often leads to the best innovations. Work with classmates, teachers, and mentors to brainstorm creative applications of AI. **Example:** Join a coding club, robotics team, or online AI community to learn from others and share your projects.

4. Advocate for Positive Change

- Use your voice to promote responsible AI development. Encourage discussions about ethics, fairness, and inclusivity in technology.

Your Imagination Shapes the Future

The future of AI isn't written yet—it's waiting for dreamers, thinkers, and doers like you to shape it. Here's how you can make an impact:

- **Solve Big Problems:** Dream of ways AI can address global challenges, like climate change, poverty, or disease.
- **Explore Creative Applications:** Use AI to create new forms of art, music, or storytelling.
- **Make AI Accessible:** Build easy-to-use tools so more people can benefit from AI regardless of their technical skills.

Every great invention starts with curiosity, creativity, and the courage to take the first step. Your ideas today could change the world tomorrow.

Revision Exercise

- Write a paragraph predicting how AI might change transportation or education in 20 years

What's Next?

Now that you've imagined the incredible possibilities AI offers, it's time to separate fact from fiction. In the next chapter, we'll tackle myths and misconceptions about AI. You'll learn what AI can truly do, what it can't, and how to see through the hype. Get ready to debunk some myths and deepen your understanding of this transformative technology!

CHAPTER 11

Debunking Myths About AI

Artificial Intelligence (AI) is one of the most transformative and talked-about technologies of our time. It's influencing everything from healthcare to entertainment, yet with all the excitement comes plenty of myths and misconceptions. Some people view AI as a magical force that can solve all problems, while others fear it will take over the world.

This chapter will help you separate fact from fiction by debunking some of the most common myths about AI.

Myth 1: AI Can Replace Humans Completely

Reality: While AI is powerful and excels at tasks involving repetitive actions or analyzing large amounts of data, it cannot replace humans in every domain. AI lacks key human traits such as creativity, empathy, and critical thinking.

Example: An AI system like AlphaZero can beat world-class chess players, but it cannot compose a sympathy, write a heartfelt novel, or solve abstract problems without human guidance. AI and humans work best when they collaborate. AI handles the data-heavy, repetitive tasks, while humans bring creativity, emotional intelligence, and ethical judgment.

Why It Matters

This myth fuels unnecessary fear about job loss and societal disruption. Instead, we should view AI as a tool that enhances human capabilities rather than replacing them.

Myth 2: AI is Always Right

Reality: AI is only as good as the data it's trained on. If that data is biased, incomplete, or incorrect, the AI's predictions or decisions will also be flawed. Blindly trusting AI can lead to serious errors.

Example: Imagine an AI-powered hiring tool trained on data from a company with a history of gender bias. The tool might favor male candidates over equally qualified female candidates, perpetuating unfair practices. Similarly, facial recognition AI can misidentify individuals, particularly from minority groups, if its training data isn't diverse enough.

Solution: Humans must remain involved to ensure AI systems are trained with balanced, high-quality data. Regular audits and ethical oversight can help minimize errors and biases.

Myth 3: AI Can Think Like Humans

Reality: AI does not think, feel, or reason like humans. It processes data and identifies patterns based on algorithms but lacks consciousness, intuition, and common sense. AI's decision-making is rooted in logic, not understanding.

Example: When you ask Siri to set a reminder, it processes your request and executes the task. While Siri might seem conversational, it doesn't "understand" what you're saying in the way a human does. It simply matches your words to pre-programmed responses and actions.

Why It Matters

Believing that AI can think like humans leads to misplaced fears about AI taking control. In reality, AI systems require clear programming and cannot act independently of their training and design.

Myth 4: AI Will Eventually Turn Against Us

Reality: This myth, popularized by movies like *The Terminator* or *The Matrix*, assumes that AI will become self-aware and develop malicious intentions. However, AI lacks desires, motivations, or goals unless explicitly programmed.

Example: An AI controlling a self-driving car follows its programming to ensure passenger safety. It doesn't "decide" to act differently because it lacks the ability to form intentions. Researchers are focused on developing AI with safety and ethical constraints to prevent misuse.

Why It Matters: These sci-fi-inspired fears distract from real concerns, such as ensuring AI systems are designed responsibly and used ethically. The goal is to create AI that aligns with human values and benefits society.

Myth 5: AI Will Take All Our Jobs

Reality: While AI will automate some tasks, it's unlikely to eliminate all jobs. Historically, new technologies have disrupted industries but also created new roles and opportunities. AI will shift the nature of work, enabling humans to focus on creative, strategic, and interpersonal tasks.

Example: Robots might assemble cars in factories, but humans are still needed to design those cars, program the robots, and ensure quality control. Similarly, AI-powered tools may handle data entry, but people are required to interpret the results and make decisions.

Solution: Workers can prepare for these changes by learning new skills, particularly in fields where human creativity and judgment are essential. Education and training programs will play a key role in helping people adapt to an AI-driven world.

Understanding AI's Limitations

Despite its impressive capabilities, AI has several limitations. Recognizing these is essential to understanding what AI can and cannot do:

Limited Creativity

AI can assist in designing or generating content, but it cannot create original ideas without human input. It relies on patterns and examples from existing data to produce outputs.

Example: An AI art generator can create images based on prompts, but it doesn't have personal inspiration or artistic intent.

Lack of Empathy

AI can detect patterns in emotions, such as identifying whether a person sounds happy or sad based on tone or text. However, it doesn't truly understand or share feelings.

Example: A chatbot might respond with, "I'm sorry you're feeling upset," but it doesn't experience empathy. This limits its ability to provide meaningful emotional support.

Dependence on Data

AI requires large datasets to learn and make predictions. If the data is incomplete, biased, or poorly labeled, the AI's performance will suffer.

Example: An AI trained on weather data from one region might perform poorly when predicting weather in a different region due to differences in climate patterns.

No Common Sense

AI lacks a basic understanding of the world, which can lead to surprising errors. It doesn't "know" anything outside of its training.

Example: An AI might misinterpret a sarcastic comment as a literal statement because it doesn't grasp context or humor.

Why Understanding AI's Capabilities and Limitations Matters

AI is a tool, not a magic solution or an existential threat. Understanding its strengths and weaknesses allows us to use it responsibly and effectively. Here's why this knowledge is crucial:

- **Informed Decision-Making:** Knowing AI's limitations prevents over-reliance and ensures better outcomes.
- **Ethical Use:** Understanding AI helps identify and mitigate potential harms, such as bias or misuse.
- **Maximizing Benefits:** By combining human creativity with AI's capabilities, we can solve complex problems and innovate in ways that benefit society.

How You Can Help Shape AI's Future

As students and future innovators, you play a vital role in guiding the development of AI. Here are some steps you can take:

1. **Stay Curious:** Keep learning about AI by exploring books, online courses, and hands-on projects.
2. **Think Critically:** Always question how AI systems work and consider their potential impact on people and society.
3. **Collaborate:** Work with others to create AI solutions that address real-world challenges.
4. **Advocate for Ethics:** Support responsible AI practices that prioritize fairness, transparency, and accountability.

Revision Exercise

- Choose one myth about AI and write a short essay explaining why it's false.

What's Next?

Now that we've debunked some myths and explored AI's limitations, you're better equipped to understand this fascinating technology. In the next chapter, we'll provide resources to help you continue your AI journey. From books and websites to online tools and courses, you'll have everything you need to keep learning and experimenting with AI. Get ready to take the next step into the future!

Learning Resources and Next Steps

Now that you have better grasp of the basics of AI, its possibilities, and its impact on our world, it's time to continue your journey with AI at a higher level. The world of AI is vast and exciting, offering endless opportunities to expand your knowledge and creativity.

In this chapter, we'll examinee some of the best books, courses, and hands-on tools to help you take the next steps in your AI adventure.

Recommended Books for Beginners

1. **"Artificial Intelligence: A Guide for Thinking Humans" by Melanie Mitchell**
   An engaging introduction that explains AI concepts in an accessible way, combining storytelling with science.

2. **"AI Superpowers" by Kai-Fu Lee**
   A fascinating exploration of AI's development, particularly in China and the US, and its potential to shape the future.

3. **"Python for Data Analysis" by Wes McKinney**
   A practical guide to using Python for data-related tasks, offering essential skills for AI and machine learning projects.

Websites and Online Courses

- **Coursera** offers a range of AI courses, including Andrew Ng's famous "Machine Learning" course for beginners.
- **Khan Academy:** Perfect for learning programming fundamentals, which are essential for AI.

- **Teachable Machine** by Google: A no-code platform to create AI models, making it a great starting point for hands-on experimentation.

YouTube Channels

1. **3Blue1Brown**
- Provides visual explanations of mathematical and AI concepts, making them easier to grasp.
2. **Sentdex**
- Focuses on practical tutorials for Python, machine learning, and real-world AI applications.
3. **Siraj Raval**
- Covers AI, deep learning, and robotics in an approachable and fun way, often with coding examples.

AI Blogs and Articles

- **Towards Data Science:** Features articles by experts on machine learning, data science, and AI ethics.
- **The Gradient:** A great resource for in-depth discussions about the latest AI research and trends.

Tips for Advancing Your AI Journey

1. Start Small and Build Gradually

- Begin with simple AI projects to reinforce what you've learned. For example, create a chatbot, an image classifier, or a mood detector.
- Gradually take on more complex projects as you become comfortable with AI tools and programming.

2. Join AI Communities

- Connect with other learners and professionals by joining platforms like **GitHub**, **Stack Overflow**, or **Reddit's AI communities**.
- Collaboration can introduce new perspectives and help you tackle challenges more effectively.

3. Experiment with AI Tools

- Explore user-friendly platforms like **Scratch** for younger learners or **RunwayML** for more advanced experimentation.
- Use tools like **Teachable Machine** to see how AI models work in real time.

4. Learn Python

- Python is the primary programming language for AI. Free resources like **Codecademy** or **Python.org** can help you master the basics.
- Once you're confident, explore libraries like **TensorFlow** and **PyTorch** for machine learning applications.

5. Stay Curious

- AI is an evolving field. Stay updated by following AI news, attending workshops, and reading about breakthroughs in research and technology.

Encouragement to Explore Robotics

AI and robotics often work hand in hand. If you've enjoyed exploring AI, then taking things a step further by studying robotics could be the perfect next step for you.

Robotics combines mechanics, electronics, and AI to create machines that can sense, move, and respond to the world around them.

Ways to Get Started in Robotics

If you like the sound of adding robotics to your AI knowledge, then these platforms below can be a good start for pursuing this knowledge:

- **LEGO Mindstorms**: Create and program robots using LEGO kits, an excellent way to learn the basics of robotics and programming.
- **Arduino:**
  This is a platform for building electronic projects, including robots. It is ideal for students who want to experiment with hardware and sensors.
- **Robotics Clubs and Competitions**: To gain hands-on experience and collaborate with others, join a local robotics group or participate in events like **FIRST Robotic**s.

The Future is Yours

AI and robotics represent two of the most transformative fields of the 21st century, and your journey is just beginning. By embracing curiosity, creativity, and collaboration, you can become an active participant in shaping the future of these technologies.

- **Start Your First Project**: Use the knowledge you've gained to build a small AI application or robot.
- **Share Your Work**: Join communities to showcase your projects and get valuable feedback.
- **Keep Learning**: Treat every project as a learning opportunity. The more you experiment, the more confident you'll become

Next Steps

1. **Select a Project:** To test your abilities, create a simple project, such as a mini-robot or chatbot.
2. **Join a Group:** Make connections with people who share your enthusiasm for robots and AI to get support and motivation.
3. **Learn Constantly:** Attend classes, read blogs, and keep up with developments in robotics and artificial intelligence.

Final Words

I appreciate you coming along on this fascinating journey into the realm of artificial intelligence. Your newly acquired skills and knowledge serve as the cornerstone of an exciting future.

The next chapter of innovation will be shaped by your ideas and inventiveness, so keep in mind that the possibilities are endless. Continue to have huge dreams and to build with courage!

Stay smart.

About The BOOK

Artificial Intelligence is no longer a distant concept from science fiction – it is shaping our daily lives, and as such cannot be overlooked as we prepare the students of today to thrive in the technological revolution. *Artificial Intelligence for Secondary Schools: A Beginner's Guide* is the perfect introduction to this fascinating field, designed specifically for young learners eager to understand and explore AI.

Written in a simple and engaging style, this book breaks down AI concepts into easily digestible sections. Readers will start by learning what AI is, how it has evolved, and how it already influences everyday activities. The book then dives into the different types of AI, how machines learn, and the essential role of data, patterns, and algorithms in making AI "smart."

For students curious about coding, this guide provides an introduction to Python, one of the most beginner-friendly programming languages, with hands-on exercises to encourage experimentation. It also explores ethical concerns surrounding AI, from bias to privacy, ensuring students understand not just how AI works but also the responsibilities that come with its use.

Beyond theory, *Artificial Intelligence for Secondary Schools* brings AI to life with real-world applications in education, healthcare, entertainment, and more. Inspiring stories of young AI innovators show that AI is not just for experts—it's a field anyone can contribute to with the right knowledge and curiosity.

About The AUTHOR

Don Mark Okonkwo is an emerging technology enthusiast and developer with a passion for exploring the transformative potential of artificial intelligence, robotics, cybersecurity, data analytics, and cryptocurrency. With a keen interest in empowering the next generation of innovators, Don combines his technical expertise with a talent for simplifying complex concepts, making cutting-edge technologies accessible to young learners.

His work reflects a deep commitment to bridging the gap between theoretical knowledge and practical application, inspiring students to embrace the technological revolution with confidence and curiosity. As a forward-thinking writer, Don is dedicated to equipping readers with the tools they need to navigate the ever-evolving digital landscape, fostering both technical skills and ethical awareness.

Artificial Intelligence for Secondary Schools: A Beginner's Guide showcases Don's ability to demystify AI and ignite a passion for innovation, making him a trusted voice in the world of technology education. Through this book, he aims to inspire students to not only understand AI but also to become active contributors to its future.

About Elegantflix Educational Project

Elegantflix Educational Project is the educational division of Elegantflix Limited, dedicated to shaping the future of education through high-quality, student-centered learning materials. We harness the expertise of seasoned subject experts and experienced teachers to create books that are not only comprehensive but also engaging, relevant, and aligned with today's educational needs.

For more educational books and resources, visit:

www.florence1billionstore.com

Or:

Scan QR Code

Elegantflix Educational Project

www.ingramcontent.com/pod-product-compliance
Lightning Source LLC
LaVergne TN
LVHW051654050326

832903LV00032B/3808